THE
POETRY & WONDERS
OF NATURE

THE
POETRY & WONDERS
OF NATURE

A COLLABORATION OF ARTS

BY

JEFF RIMLAND

AND

JOHN P. CARDONE

Authors' Notes:

Cover elephant photo by: Kieran O'Keefe
Back cover Jeff Rimland photo by: Angela J. Rimland
Back cover John P. Cardone photo by: Kathy Cardone

All interior photos by: Author John P. Cardone unless otherwise mentioned

Graphics and design by: Author John P. Cardone

Anyone interested in obtaining a professionally printed and matted photograph or a reproduction of any of the poems in this book, contact the authors via email for more details.

To contact the authors, email:

Jeff Rimland: Jeffrimland@msn.com
John P. Cardone: WaterviewsArts@aol.com

Published by: Waterviews Arts

ISBN (paperback) 979-8-218-42546-3
ISBN (eBook) 979-8-218-42547-0

To order additional copies of this book contact the publisher:
WaterviewsArts@aol.com

DEDICATION

This book celebrates the conservation organizations around the world—for all that they do for our planet.

TABLE OF CONTENTS

FOREWORD

by former Suffolk County, New York and present Volusia County, Florida Poet Laureate Dr. David B. Axelrod

Why not have the best of both worlds? If a picture is worth a thousand words, then why not also have poems which refine language to just the right number of words to enhance the images? As much as we experience the world through our eyes, we are language creatures craving information that allows us to organize life. Jeff Rimland's creations have the rare ability to make facts feel "poetic." So many poets feel they must slave to be imagistic. Some even invent ekphrastic poems—poems that try to describe a painting or a photograph. Why would we need to do that? We have the actual images—in this case, John P. Cardone's artful nature photographs.

Jeff has created poetry that can stand on its own. John, in the tradition of photographers like Ansel Adams, doesn't just tease us or make us wish we were there to view the subject of the photos—the photos are the thing; the photos are the art itself.

In this book, *The Poetry & Wonders of Nature*, we experience and can even give a name to a new artform—the merger of art photography and facts rendered as poetry. Factual, journalistic prose that reads like fiction has been called "Faction." Here we have "Factography"—the blend of photos and factual poetry.

Jeff and John, these clever comrades in arts, exemplify the virtues of Factography. Just note some wonderful creations, as on page 4, where "Eternity" prompts us to "press our feet into the sand" and get grounded as we understand that "there are more oceans than land." Rather than succumb to moments "fraught with fear," we use Jeff's wise percepts and "realize the eternity of the waves and realize we are eternal, too."

On page 6, "The Visit" of a hummingbird paradoxically becomes the photographer's focal point and a poet's moment floating in time—despite "day[s] of issues needing attention." Through the collaboration of the authors, this book itself becomes not just an artifact on a coffee table, but a place to escape and calm oneself. Sit with the book, live in the book. Experience the joy.

On page 8, "Staring Eyes" are not just sometimes fatal and frozen moments of a deer in the headlights, but a moment of contemplation and communion when we might otherwise be "on high alert." Reading ahead in the book, on page 10, we transition to snow-covered mountains and a lifetime that is "proof that I [we] can climb."

Poetry, photography, and art sometimes dwell in ambiguity devolving into despair. For that reason, it's great that such seriousness can also contain a sense of humor. What would we have without references to Alvin and the Chipmunks or such moral exemplars as Bugs Bunny and Woody Woodpecker? We who own this book certainly don't want it to be "That's all Folks." More, more.

INTRODUCTION
by John P. Cardone

Have you ever wondered about the artist's mind? How one artist, say a painter, sees the subject in his/her mind as he puts paint on a canvas with a brush. Or how the mind of a sculptor, who chisels and carves away on a block of wood or stone, reveals a subject's form and beauty. Or the nature photographer, who spends countless hours of time observing wildlife, deciding how the subject image should be captured and composed in the mind's eye even before raising a camera. Or the singer-songwriter, who sitting at a keyboard or strumming a guitar, can use imagination to create tunes that comfort or give joy to life. Or the poet, who may be inspired by a life event or a visual, puts to paper these feelings with rhyming or free-verse lyrics, lines of words that may make the reader give pause at its meaning and beauty.

While they have different mindsets, there are things they agree on—that the art they are about to create starts with inspiration, settles for a while in emotion, and leaves them overflowing with passion. That's why they do it—for the love of creating.

What about the non-artistic mind—is there such a thing, and can you compare the two minds? Research studies have been fascinating in this regard. The difference literally lies in the structure and functioning of the brain. Because of these differences, artists see the world differently. Art professors have long maintained that training students to see the world in a different way is critical to their development as an artist. The many differences could be inborn and passed along in genes at birth, or (the good news) could be developed in life from exposure to training.

I have often thought of poems about nature as a great match for my wildlife and waterscape photos and descriptions. So, when my friend and fellow author, Jeff Rimland, asked if I would be interested in developing a book of poems and photographs on nature subjects, I jumped at the opportunity. Actually, I had thought about doing the same thing plus adding descriptions, too. We laughed at the coincidence of these ideas during the discussion.

A poet may have an experience in nature or observe scenes of nature and, in their mind, hear words of wonder and amazement. Wildlife and flora, landscape and waterscape views can create thoughts that become words, phrases, and concepts on paper. Most often a very personal approach—something from the heart. Nature sightings create images in the photographer's mind—colors, shapes, sizes, and behavior that in their final results at an art show often have people exclaiming, "Wow."

While both surrender to moments of inspiration in different forms, the results speak of beauty, capturing action. But in the end, they merge to inspire people of all ages to spend time in nature and come to see the wonders—you just have to spend time and observe. That's our goal with the creation of this book, *The Poetry & Wonders of Nature: A Collaboration of Arts.*

A funny thing happened during the process of writing this book. We frequently sent each other short drafts of our work, and seeing things develop excited and motivated us to keep going, to keep creating. It was both joyous and inspiring.

One interesting experience I had occurred back in the summer of 2023, during an unexpected hospitalization to treat and manage a sudden, troublesome, and dangerous drop in my platelet cell counts—to unsafe levels. Remember I'm a two-time cancer survivor. I found myself using mindfulness techniques to switch my thoughts away from my health troubles by viewing my nature photographs and writing about nature. It worked. As a matter of fact, I developed most of this introduction and organized other sections during those days in the hospital. If readers are interested in how nature subjects are perfect for being mindful, may I suggest my books *The Healing Power of Nature* and *Chronicles of a Nature Photographer* for more details, samples of scientific studies, and examples of powerful photo images.

Meanwhile, I hope you find our collaboration to be motivating and move you to explore nature around you and to visit the many places that offer wonderful nature experiences. The contents of this book were created for any age, even for children, for they are nature sponges soaking it all in. There are thirty-six nature subjects in this edition; from inspiring wildlife, to beautiful landscape and waterscape scenes, to gorgeous gardens, to some well-known locations, and to others you may not have heard about. Of course, there are backyards and local parks included—for, as they say, there's no place like home. Each section includes one or more photographs of the subject so you can see the sights seen in nature. These are followed by an explanation of the subjects. You'll enjoy the nature features, interesting facts, locations, and descriptions. On the facing pages, poet Jeff Rimland gives us all a gift of his free-verse poems that sometimes reflect his personal opinions, which are often an emotional reaction, or a shared experience, or his special way he describes the beauty and calmness of nature. He offers more details about this in the following "Preface" written for this book.

For those readers interested in more information, you will find our "References and Resources" sections to be helpful. There is also a blank page at the back of the book on page 90 for note-taking or to write comments you might want to recall. As authors, we welcome comments and questions from our readers. Contact details are provided on page iv. We appreciate your positive review mentions and ask that you share these with your friends and family via Facebook, Amazon reviews, and on your social media platforms. Join us in our mission to get people to spend more time out in nature. So, read on and enjoy.

Fondly,

John P. Cardone

Blank Page (con't)

PREFACE
by Jeff Rimland

When deciding to write a book on nature, wildlife, and poetry, a collaboration of arts was formed between myself and John P. Cardone: author, nature photographer, and naturalist. The concept of creating a book about nature and wildlife with my poetry is an outcrop of my other five books of poetry. My poetry has always been about feelings and thoughts about history, loss, love, irony, and nostalgia, which have appealed to many different people. *The Poetry & Wonders of Nature* also expresses the human emotion behind nature and wildlife and, in many cases, extinction. We dedicate this book to the conservancy population who can review the descriptions, photos, and poetry of nature and wildlife, helping to create meaning in saving the planet.

The poetry in this volume represents my feelings and thoughts in my mind's eye, the minds of friends, and the public viewpoint. The poems' meanings can vary from how they apply to the world now, how they applied to prehistoric times, and how they interrelate into history, biology, paleontology, and my own feelings and interpretations. Readers should deeply contemplate that wildlife and nature influence the psyche. You should care because wildlife and nature are part of your world, affecting individuals in the present day, and will affect future generations.

As an author, I am always looking for creative ways to write on various subjects. When I undertook this project, it was difficult to write "on-demand" poetry, but I was able to master it to some degree by doing research. I read and re-read John Cardone's descriptions of the wildlife and nature subjects, checking research sources online, gaining clarity on biology, nature, paleontology, and cultural aspects of nature and wildlife to write poems on every subject in the book. Further, I utilized several of my personal experiences with certain wildlife and nature subjects to also write some of the poems. It was very enlightening to me as an author to be able to write these thirty-six poems about nature and wildlife subjects. The poetry, descriptions, and photos in *The Poetry & Wonders of Nature* make this a unique collaboration of the arts.

Warm Regards,

Jeff Rimland

American Bald Eagle

The American bald eagle has the distinction of being the national bird of the United States, adopted in 1792. It is the country's proudest symbol, recognized everywhere. It is estimated that the bald eagle population in the United States numbers more than 316,700. During the 1700s and early 1800s, bald eagles were a dying breed. Farmers saw them as pests and they were frequently shot. Deforestation led to a reduction of the forests where they lived. The chemical DDT, introduced in the 1940s, poisoned the fish that the eagles ate. The Bald Eagle Protection Act, introduced around that time, turned the tide on a dwindling bald eagle population.

Here are some interesting American bald eagle facts: Adult bald eagles can grow to reach two-and-a-half to three feet tall and weigh an average of seven to fourteen pounds. Their wingspans are usually six to seven-and-a-half feet. In the wild, bald eagles can live to be twenty years old. Eagles build the largest bird nests, up to thirteen feet deep and six to eight feet wide.

Our Symbol

The symbol of our country.
Strength, boldness.
Taking so many weeks to find the nest,
worth capturing:
in a photographic portrait,
in its natural habitat

The American bald eagle's extinction status and its recovery
at the beginning of our nation's history,
taking so many years to reclaim our birthright,
is much like our country today—
always coming back from the brink.

Soaring through the heavens, over the mountaintops,
swirling around the river valleys, up through the canyons,
never faulting.

As in everything American,
bald eagles build the biggest nests.
Snatching fish and small critters,
soaring away to feed their young.

Whether in politics, personal freedoms, social justice,
international affairs, or economics,
the U.S. has always spread its wings and flown far and wide,
showing its boldness and strength

The symbol of our country,
the American bald eagle shows the way forward.

Ocean Waves

On an ordinary day, people are mesmerized by the power and beauty of waves. They frequently walk the beach, watching and listening to the sounds as waves crash onto the beach. When the summer sun brings people out to the ocean beaches, they might just sit and enjoy the show. Yet, on other days, people around the world paddle out to the breakers and, when ready, stand on a fiberglass board to ride a wave as it roars to the shore. Then again, during a storm, we fear the destructive intensity of waves as they slam into our shores, eroding the beaches and flooding beachfront homes, causing millions of dollars in damage.

Ocean waves are generated by the surface wind and together combine their energy into uncontrollable elements of Mother Nature. Two other sources of waves are standing waves and seismic waves which can be found in open bays or brought on by tsunamis respectively.

Average ocean waves can be as small as a foot in height on calm days to waves up to one hundred feet tall when the wind is blowing. Waves during a storm such as a hurricane can be enormous. Another factor that influences waves is ocean tides. During high tides, waves can be larger than normal. Locations around the world that have the largest waves can be found in Nazaré, Portugal; Puerto Escondido, Mexico; Oahu, Hawaii; Cortes Bank, California; Western Australia; and Teahupo'o, Tahiti.

Eternity

Pressing our feet into the sand,
watching the waves push through the whitecaps,
smooth out and settle on the shore.

Realizing that on Earth there are more oceans than land,
still not knowing all about them,
exploration of the oceans—
an outcrop of my fascination
with nature and wildlife.

There is beauty in the ocean waves,
and there are moments fraught with fear,
in tidal waves from tsunamis.

We are walking the beach,
seeing a ship on the horizon,
showing more waves and
just standing there contemplating;

Our past, our future.
We realize the eternality of the waves,
and how we are eternal, too.

Beloved Hummingbirds

Hummingbirds are elusive birds and at two-and-a-half to three-and-a-half inches in size, they are not easy to spot. Hummers have movements that astound. They can fly vertically, backward, and even upside down. They can also hover. As a result, if they are feeding, they fly in spurts, darting from one flower to another in unexpected patterns. They move slower around nectar feeders, most likely because the feeders provide a good amount of food. They flap their wings fifty to sixty times per second and up to eighty times when hovering, which causes the hum one might hear. While there are over 350 hummingbird species worldwide, here on Long Island, New York, we only have one type of hummingbird: the ruby-throated hummingbird, and only the mature male has the red throat. Mention hummingbirds, and you'll find people smiling. They truly are a beloved species of birds.

The migration pattern of the ruby-throated hummingbird is fascinating. In the spring they travel north, finding food sources on the journey. They can travel as much as twenty-three miles in one day, frequently returning to their favorite nesting sites. During the warm days, hummers will locate their favorite flowers and feeders. However, once the cold weather moves in, they begin their return migration to the south in early or mid-September. Their one-way travel is as much as 1,200 miles to Mexico and South America.

The Visit

One of the smallest birds
but larger than life.
Symbol of recovery and healing,
connected with me somehow,
on some spiritual level.

The visit was miraculous.
Coincidence,
seeing my beloved hummingbird
every day hovering and hovering,
to spread seeds, pollen; life itself.

Usually found in Mexico, South America,
nature preserves, and fields,
made an appearance in my backyard
at a key time in my life,
hovering and hovering,
perhaps waiting until I return.

Returning from a day of introspection,
and delight
Returning from a day of issues,
needing attention,
Returning from a day of teaching,
photography, and nature.
Returning from a day . . .
and it hasn't left since.

White-Tailed Deer

The white-tailed deer is a large mammal fairly common in North America, including Long Island, New York. People either like watching them roam free or hate them because they are known to carry ticks and eat plants and trees around homes. While white-tailed deer are primarily nocturnal, favoring the hours of dusk and dawn to search for food, they do however venture out during daylight. The male deer can range in weight from 150 to 300 pounds, while the female weight ranges from 88 to 200 pounds.

During the spring and summer, the deer's coat is a reddish-brown color but turns more gray-brown during the fall and winter. The main identifying detail is the deer's white tail. When alarmed by a predator, the deer will raise its tail as a warning. When threatened, the white-tail deer will bolt at a fast gallop. They are a beautiful sight as they leap over brush or downed logs.

Staring Eyes

Deer in the woods
this morning,
staring directly at me.

Somehow,
reaches me specifically.
Alerting me of their presence,
as they are on high alert
themselves.

Prancing through the forest near my home,
a fawn followed by its mother, I suppose,
stop and stare at me again.
Alerting me of their presence,
as they are on high alert
themselves.

As they seem to do this,
off and on,
makes me wonder:
How long have they done this,
and who have they met with their eyes,
and how long ago it started.

Snow-Covered Mountains

Seeing mountain ranges anywhere in the world can be breathtaking. However, when snow-covered, they can also be inspiring. In the United States, the location with the most snow-covered mountains is Washington State—Mount Baker and Mount Rainier are among the places with the most snow. The tallest mountain range in the world is Mount Everest, located in Nepal and China, at 29,035 feet. When a mountain is only partially covered with snow, it is considered snow-capped.

Pictured above, views of the Rocky Mountain National Park in Colorado show the snow-covered mountains' scenic beauty. Whether hiking, snowshoeing, or skiing, being within such magnificence is humbling.

Snow-Covered Challenge

Majestic in its beauty.
Taking to the mountains,
and snowcapped,
doubly humbled by sheer size.

Challenged by its terrain:
walking where pioneers walked.
Pursuing a dream of mine,
climbing a mountain,
no matter how large or small,
proving to myself that I can do anything
I put my mind to.

Climbing mountains my whole life.
Figurative mountains of childhood,
teen years, family life, love life, marriage,
career, and parenthood have been met with
tribulations and success.

Proof that I can climb it,
pursue my dreams and persevere
where many have not.

Sunrise

The photo of a sunrise above was taken while kayaking the Carman's River in Shirley, Long Island, New York. What I remember most was the eerie quiet and the speed at which the sun rose in the sky. Seeing the morning glow light up the shoreline reminded me why photographers refer to this time as the golden hour.

There's a calmness to the morning sun that is not felt at any other time. A rising sun gives one a feeling of hope, knowing that another new day is born. It is full of promise of what is to come while having deep feelings of being alive.

Two other magnificent sunrise locations were standing at the shore on Maui in Hawaii and sitting on a boulder atop Cadillac Mountain, Acadia National Park in Maine; both breathtaking views.

Here are two favorite sunrise quotes…

"The secret to a good morning is to watch the sunrise with an open heart." — Anthony T. Hincks

"Every sunrise is a poem written on the earth with words of light, warmth, and love." — Debasish Mridha

Sunrise to a New Day

On the horizon,
it is a stark darkness
until that split second—
the light peeks through,
raising ever so slowly, it seems.
But before long,
the sun rises high above the horizon,
preparing us for the day ahead.

In the rainforests,
species react to their internal clocks.
On the prairies and the deserts
sunrise signifies the start of a new day.
In the snowy highlands—
the sun peeks over the mountaintops.

Wherever you are in the world, in the United States, Asia,
Australia, Europe, Russia, Ukraine, and even Antarctica,
the sun rises, continuing your day,
in your way,
perhaps signifying the ability to fight another day—
whether it is war
or your personal battles
of love and life.

Ospreys in Flight

Ospreys are part of the hawk family and are nicknamed "fish-hawks" because of their fish-based diet. In some seashore locations, they are called "seahawks." Ospreys have an unusual ability to catch fish. They dive into the water with their wings tucked back along their sides and their talons positioned out in front of their heads. The dive, feet first, is so forceful they become completely submerged. The osprey is a large raptor, reaching some two feet in length with an average wingspan of fifty-nine to seventy inches. They can weigh three to four pounds. Interestingly, ospreys mate for life—usually returning to the same nest as the year before.

North American osprey populations became endangered in the 1950s due to chemical pollutants such as DDT, which thinned their eggshells and hampered reproduction. Ospreys have rebounded significantly in recent decades, though they remain scarce in some locales. Ospreys are migratory. While they spend months in the warm weather of North America, once the cold weather takes hold, they will fly as much as 6,000 miles to spend the winter in Central and South America. Some will winter in the southernmost United States, including parts of Florida and California. One could say, they are true snowbirds.

Swooping In

Nesting their young
year after year, after year, after year.
Teaching their young how to fly.
Flying from the nest,
swooping up and down,
far and wide.
Swooping and angling down,
spotting fish,
swooping into the water,
catching the fleeing fish,
dropping it into the nest.

The flight of the osprey,
the seahawk, majestic in its appearance:
the wingspan is impressive.
Thinking that birds are descendant from the dinosaur
makes me wonder in an existential way;

Where we come from,
where are we going?
Let's see where we can fly,
to truly see what the future holds.

Rivers

Rivers can be found all around the globe. They were created almost exclusively by the movement of the glaciers during the end of the Ice Age. There are four types of rivers: permanent, periodic, episodic, and exotic. Permanent rivers have water all year round. Periodic rivers run dry on occasion, usually located in arid climates where evaporation is greater than precipitation. Episodic rivers are rarely occurring rivers formed from run-off channels in very dry regions. Exotic rivers are rivers that flow through arid (desert) regions.

The water in most rivers within North America comes from melting snow and rain in the mountain areas such as those found in Colorado, Pennsylvania, and upstate New York. On Long Island, New York, a geographic location without mountains, river water is derived from rain and underground aquifers, as well as from lakes and ponds.

While many rivers, such as the Mississippi River, facilitate transportation, most smaller rivers in the United States have become recreational areas and the surrounding lands are home to an abundance of wildlife.

My River

So many years ago,
discovering a river near my home,
watching it wind down and passing by,
turn by turn around the bend,
spotting wildlife and capturing many photos.
It became my river over the years.

Drifting down my river,
the stresses of body and mind left behind,
moving forward and forward.
Stopping to see all the wildlife,
amazing wildlife,
showing me the extent of species unknown to me,
or species known far away,
but are now here locally.

As I paddled close to shore,
seeing water birds
and woodpeckers
developing their nests,
and perhaps,
creating secret hiding places.

Skimming the riverbank, there is a path
from the shore into the woods;
seeing myself spreading out a blanket
and laying there, contemplating.
Drifting down my river,
leaving the stresses of body and mind behind,
realizing that there is always
the river, my river,
to comfort and inspire me.

Monarch Butterflies

In the insect world, there are many wonderful subjects to photograph. However, none are more treasured than the monarch butterfly. This can be attributed to two factors: first, its beauty, and second, its story-like migration. In general, people, especially children, love the monarch butterfly. After all, what's not to love? Monarchs are large butterflies with a wingspan of three to four inches. Their bright orange wings are outlined with black borders that include white dots throughout. Black veins divide sections of the wings that seem to accent its look. The underside of each wing has a more pale orange coloring that adds contrast to its beauty.

Monarch butterflies are found across North America wherever suitable feeding, breeding, and overwintering habitat exists. Monarchs are known to migrate as much as thousands of miles from the United States and Canada south to California and Mexico during the winter months. The migration is considered one of nature's spectacular phenomena since they journey using an internal compass that points them in the correct direction.

The Monarch

The king has spoken.
The prince of orange, too.
Colors of the monarch-
butterfly.

Loveliness,
beauty to all.
Especially to children.

Floating above colorful flowers,
its vision like human,
recognizing their nectar nourishment.

Having a miraculous internal clock,
to travel south and southwest
during the east and north winters.

How is it possible,
from egg to larva to pupa, and to adult?
All this with the internal clock.
Who or what devised this clock?
Can we see it if we look?
This is the mystery of the monarch butterfly,
for which we may never know the answer.

Woodpeckers

There are 239 species of woodpeckers in the world. In the Continental United States, there are twenty-three species and in New York state, only eleven. Long Island has six types of woodpeckers. An odd fact about the woodpeckers found on Long Island is that five of the six have some combination of white, black, and red in their coloring. The sixth, the northern flicker (seen in left photo), has more of a brownish coloring.

Observing a woodpecker land on a tree trunk illustrates the amazing marvels found in nature. Most birds land on tree branches where they can balance and hold on. Woodpeckers have the uncanny ability to cling to the trunk without falling to the ground. In addition to their feet, they use their tails as a way of steadying themselves.

Woodpeckers' feet have an amazing biology. They consist of four toes: the first and the fourth face backward, and the second and third face forward. This foot arrangement is ideal for grasping the limbs and trunks of trees. Most woodpeckers can walk vertically up a tree trunk, and even walk down. This ability is useful when foraging for food or nest building. Woodpeckers have strong bills that they use for drilling and drumming on trees, and long, sticky tongues for extracting food (insects and larvae). Woodpecker bills are typically longer, sharper, and stronger than the bills of other birds.

Woody

Woody was his name:
Woody the Woodpecker;
the cartoon character
was all we knew of woodpeckers.
We didn't know its tools,
its opposing feet,
its sticky tongue,
its strong, sharp bills
but no silly laugh.

As the woodpecker forages
for flying insects, ants, termites, caterpillars, and spiders,
protecting us from infestations,
they bore holes into the trees.
They live
where the insects live—
deep inside, rings, and rings.

As the woodpecker
drills and drills,
echoing with reverberations,
deep within the forest,
we realize
that the woodpecker,
the *genus picus*,
has been doing all this
for the last 23 million years.

Assateague Ponies

Watching the ponies of Assateague Island roam free, one can get an idea of what nature was like before civilization changed the world. These ponies are an actual breed—not young horses that will grow. The classification of horse versus pony is determined by size measured from the ground to its withers. To be a pony, it has to fall below fifty-eight inches.

Assateague Island is a narrow barrier island thirty-seven miles long, consisting of nearly 42,000 acres. The largest portion, about two-thirds of the northern island, is in Maryland, while the smaller portion, the southern third, is in the state of Virginia. The island is located off the eastern coast of the Delmarva Peninsula facing the Atlantic Ocean. On the other side, Assateague Bay separates the island from the mainland.

The ponies of Assateague Island have an interesting history. Part of that history is the local folklore that the first ponies to arrive were survivors of a Spanish galleon shipwreck off the coast of Virginia in 1750. However, since there is no evidence of the incident, historians explain that it is more likely that the descendants of these ponies were brought to the barrier islands in the 17th century by owners on the mainland to avoid livestock taxation.

Running Wild

Wild, wild horses
could not keep me from basking in their beauty.

Ponies that are a separate breed, not just small horses,
they've lived on the island for hundreds of years
not really knowing how they arrived.

Dozens of ponies, herding together and running together.
Spreading out into small packs,
settling down to feed,
then coming over to me as my camera snaps their photo,
capturing their fierceness,
their vulnerability.

Afterward, herding together and running together,
seeming to show happiness beyond compare.
Taking the boat back to the mainland,
I ponder—
pondering the Assateague ponies'
place in the world.

The Beautiful Mute Swan

Mute swans were imported to North America from Europe in the mid-1800s through the early 1900s. They are among the largest birds and can be very aggressive when protecting their young and nesting areas. They are called mute because they are quieter than other species of swans. Mute swans can grow to fifty-five to sixty-three inches long, weigh up to twenty to thirty-two pounds, and have a wingspan of eighty to ninety-five inches.

There are three types of swans found in North America: trumpeter swan, the tundra swan, and the mute swan. Mute swans can be identified by their white plumage and orange beak, which is bordered with black. The mute swan's diet consists mostly of aquatic vegetation found in the waterways and along the grassy shore of their habitat. They are voracious eaters and will consume up to eight pounds per day. This is one of the problems with this non-native species of swans—they consume more vegetation than can grow back.

The beauty of the mute swan is frequently mirrored in Russian ballets and is described in European fairy tales. In Hans Christian Andersen's fairy tale, *The Ugly Duckling*, one egg hatches an odd-looking bird that then grows to be a beautiful swan.

The Ugly Duckling

The mute swan
is the quiet swan.
Much quieter than any other swan.

It's also the largest swan,
eating and eating and eating,
further eliminating the overgrowth.

The mute swan
is also the fiercest swan
when protecting its young
in its nest, which they use
over and over and over again.

The mute swan is a symbol:
watching it elegantly paddling in the water,
making us optimistic
since, at one time, it was
an ugly duckling.

Canada Geese

Canada geese are large waterbirds with long necks, large bodies, big webbed feet, and wide, flat bills. Often misnamed as "Canadian" geese, the correct name is *Canada* geese (plural) or *Canada* goose (singular). While slightly smaller than a mute swan, a male Canada goose can be between twenty-nine to forty-three inches in length, weighing from five to fourteen pounds with a wingspan of fifty to sixty-seven inches. The female goose is somewhat lighter. Another interesting fact is that Canada geese mate for life which can be as long as ten to twenty-five years.

Native to North America, Canada geese can be found on or close to fresh water; the Canada goose is also common in brackish waters found within estuaries, marshes, and lagoons. One interesting trait of Canada geese is the fact that if they are flying toward you, you'll most likely hear their loud honking call before you see them. And if they land on the water, they make a big splash on the move until they come to a stop. Because of the sound they make, Canada geese are nicknamed "honkers."

The Honker

Flying in V formation,
unconscious rotation to the front,
honking and honking and honking.
Hearing them before you see them.

Feeding time, asking humans for food.
North America is their home,
but Europe, Australia, and New Zealand
have been claimed as home to many flocks.

Time to mate,
Canada geese partner for life.
Living between 10 and 25 years
among human constructs like parking lots
and camping sites.

Environmentally, the population is increasing;
their excrement is leading to be known as pests,
and aircraft strikes are causing a decrease in air safety
and a potential decrease in human population.

Harbor Seals

Harbor seals migrate from their iced-over winter habitats in the north to the warmer climate of the coastal areas of New England and New York—they seem to really enjoy visiting Long Island. Male harbor seals generally grow to five to five-and-a-half feet in length, weighing 300 to 350 pounds, while the smaller females reach approximately four-and-a-half to five feet, weighing 150 to 240 pounds. Harbor seals are thought to live for at least thirty years. Harbor seals feed on fish, shellfish, and crustaceans.

In order to bask in the sun and rest, harbor seals will "haul out"—a term that means to pull themselves up on shoreline rocks exposed during low tides. Often, while resting, the harbor seal will take on a banana-shaped profile that is unique to harbor seals with both their tail and head raised off the rocks. They have a dog-like snout and a rounded face that makes them appear cute to people watching them. While taking photographs from a distance, harbor seals seem to pose for the camera, turning their heads and making faces.

That Face

That Face:
the mustache whiskers,
the piercing eyes.

Resting in the sun,
on rocks,
posing for the camera
in Shinnecock Inlet
in Southampton.

Hard to imagine
they're stalking their prey using those whiskers
in dark murky waters,
keep hunting in packs
where their prey is salmon and herring,
captured and eaten whole.

Just goes to show you,
like judging a book by its cover—
The cute face to humans
is deceiving
when it comes to the animal kingdom.

Blue Jays

Not to be mistaken with the Toronto Blue Jays baseball team, the blue jay bird is a large songbird found in eastern North America living in most of the eastern and central United States. Blue jays are very common in New York, including the backyards of homes on Long Island. Some blue jays migrate during the winter to warmer locations while many do not. The blue jay is a colorful, noisy bird that can appear aggressive to protect their food and young. Adult blue jays grow to be nine-and-a-half to twelve inches in length with an average wingspan of thirteen to seventeen inches. Their diet includes acorns, insects, and sunflower seeds, as well as wild berries. They are attracted to backyard birdbaths as a source of drinking water and cooling baths during the hot summer months.

Interestingly enough, there is a species of jay called Canada jay and another found in Midwestern states called the gray jay as seen above (upper right). Gray jays can be found south of the Rocky Mountains to Arizona and New Mexico. Some say they are the same species, while other experts describe them as different.

Blue jays have a beautiful blue, white, and black coloring that stands out brightly.

Loyalty

The blue jay
Symbol of good luck,
symbol of future loyalties
in love.

The blue jay.
True blue,
symbolizes their loyalty,
as they mate for life.

The blue jay
protects its food and its young
in the midst of the soft feature of loyalty.

The blue jay symbolizes the love you desire,
even if you don't have that love yet.
The blue jay symbolizes judgment,
questioning who is judging you,
even if it's you.

The blue jay symbolizes
hope for the future
which we all need from the universe.

The Insect World

There might not be another subject in nature that is as wonderous as the insect world—small subjects that make big statements. There are more than a million described species in the world—18,000 insect species live in North America. Insects inhabit a wide variety of habitats and display extraordinary diversity in size, behavior, structure, and color. Insects are mostly solitary, but some, such as certain bees, ants, and termites, are social and live in large, well-organized colonies.

Insect pollinators are essential to the life cycle of many flowering plant species on which most organisms, including humans, are at least partly dependent; without them, the terrestrial portion of the biosphere would be devastated. Many insects are considered ecologically beneficial as predators, and a few provide direct economic benefits. Silkworms produce silk and honeybees produce honey, and both have been domesticated by humans.

Insects are great photography subjects considering their varying size and coloring. This is illustrated in the three photos above—a dragonfly, a water spider, and a grasshopper.

Perhaps Just Like Us

Crawling across their acres,
our inches, their feet,
making their way
across a brick, cement block, a forest floor,
a tile floor.

Flying across the room, across a leaf,
across a desert sandbox.
These amazing creatures . . .
Some have social constructs,
like ants and bees,
termites and wasps.

The queens,
workers, and soldiers:
reproduction, caring for the young,
food collection, nest construction,
and defending the colony.

Amazingly, they seem familiar.
Each in our different dimensions,
we don't think they can see us,
but they somehow sense us.

When we've been stung,
when we swat the fly away,
when they swarm and we water them down, eradicating them.
When we walk on them as they climb out of their ant hills,
they sense us,
as we sense the hurricane and tornado.

How different are they from us?

Chipmunks

Chipmunks are energetic and speedy critters. They are small members of the squirrel family with a total of twenty-five different species. Within this family there are three main categories: Tamias (eastern North America), Neotamias (western North America), and Eutamias (Eurasia). Their pudgy cheeks, glossy eyes, stripes, and bushy tails have made them a favorite among cartoon animators, which landed them a series of starring roles in Hollywood. The three most well-known animated singing chipmunks are Alvin, Simon, and Theodore.

Chipmunks have a pointed muzzle, prominent ears, and small eyes set on the sides of their heads. Although a chipmunk's mouth is small, their cheek pouches can expand up to three times the size of their head. Chipmunks have a varied omnivorous diet mainly consisting of nuts, fruits, seeds, berries, grains, bird eggs, small frogs, fungi, insects, and worms. Food is stuffed into their large cheek pouches and carried back to store in their dens. Chipmunks are solitary animals, and male and female do not pair until breeding season. Although chipmunks hibernate from late autumn until early spring, they do not store fat; instead, they slowly gnaw away at their supplies throughout the winter, waking every two weeks or so to eat.

Alvin

We know chipmunks from
Alvin, Simon, and Theodore.
When they sing the Christmas songs,
when they take a road trip,
when they don't know where they are.

Sleeping fifteen hours a day,
prey for many animals,
and predatory themselves.

Burrowing underground,
sometimes as deep as eleven feet,
eating what they store
in the wintertime,
hibernating,
waking every two weeks to eat.

Fully grown in six weeks,
they leave the burrow two weeks later.
Prey for many animals,
and predatory themselves;

chipmunks sadly only live three years.

Our Colorful Flowers

If asked, most people would say that they couldn't imagine a world without flowers. For the most part, they are all around us. So much so, that we may not always see them. Yet, they add beauty and color to our home gardens, make for great romantic gifts, ease our pain at funerals, and on the business side feed an estimated 36 billion-dollar global cut flower industry in 2022.

In the United States, there are numerous gardens that attract tourists: Busch Gardens in Tampa Bay, Florida; New York Botanical Gardens in New York City; San Francisco Botanical Gardens in California to name a few. Here on Long Island, New York, some of the most beautiful arboretums and nurseries include Westbury Gardens, Planting Fields Arboretum in Oyster Bay, and Bayard Cutting Arboretum in Great River. People delight in gardening as a joyful hobby around their homes. Gardening can be a meditation activity, a way to exercise joints and muscles, and it provides a positive effect on mood and emotions, as well as calming stressed-out minds when observing the results of their labors.

Flowers are a most important part of our natural world. Plants act as highly effective air cleaners, absorbing carbon dioxide plus many air pollutants, while releasing clean oxygen. In short, they help make our planet habitable.

Glory

Smell their aroma,
feast on their exotica.
Their part in healing,
so many types.

Meanings are fascinating.
There is the anemone or windflower.
There is amaryllis or sparkle.
There are chrysanthemums or gold flowers.
There is the daisy or days eye,
and there is the forget-me-not, so the lover is never forgotten.

Wandering the garden's bright colors,
and birds singing.
Viewing dirt paths, rocks,
bees buzzing, pollen-filled flowers.

Bringing me peace
in the garden,
it's important to take note:
its glory can make a difference.

Meanings are fascinating.
Colors are glorious,
healing can take place.
Smell them regularly.

Amazing Turtles

There are over 310 species of turtles in the world, and they can be divided into three major groups: tortoises (mostly land-based), terrapins (freshwater turtles), and marine turtles (also called sea turtles). Within New York state, there are twenty turtle species listed on the NYS DEC list. On Long Island, the number is closer to ten. Most frequently, I spot freshwater turtles while hiking and kayaking Long Island. Out on the Great South Bay, and mostly near the reeds along the shore, I have spotted sea turtles such as the leatherback and the Kemp's ridley.

Turtles are reptiles that either live on the land (terrestrial) or live in the water (aquatic). Some turtles live in both environments—land and water. Based on turtle fossils found by scientists, it appears that they have been around for 220 million years—longer than snakes, lizards, and dinosaurs.

Turtles can be seen lying on a downed log, swimming, digging themselves into the mud, climbing up a shore, or strolling across the grass. Turtles love to bask in the sun, but the reasons they sun themselves are lifesaving. One reason is to absorb Ultraviolet B radiation which helps with the production of Vitamin D3, plus turtles are cold-blooded, and the sun helps turtles regulate their body temperature. It's interesting that turtles, who appear slow and clunky on land, can seem so balletic while swimming—graceful as can be and very entertaining.

Slow and Steady

Their shell, its own house,
as they live on land
and sea,
under the ocean for hours.
Godlike to Vishnu,
carrying the world on its back.
Symbol of Enki.
Sacred animals in Confucianism.
Center of creation stories.

Humans killing them over the centuries,
and thousands of years,
eating their eggs, their bodies,
making soup,
causing species to become extinct.

Turtles still live though,
after millions of years,
much like in the Aesop fable;

Slow and steady wins the race.

The Last Day of Summer

On the calendar, the last day of summer is not noted, and it is mostly not celebrated. While the summer solstice, the first day of summer, is significant because it is Earth's longest day, the actual end of summer seems less important.

The photo above was taken on the last day of summer on a foggy, misty morning while kayaking the Carman's River in Brookhaven, New York. As a nature lover, to me, the look of the flowers symbolizes the end of warm days and the start of the colder months to come. In nature, the end of summer means the days will be getting shorter, and the nights will be getting longer. In the bird world, it won't be long before the cooler weather signals a start to the winter migration.

While summertime is a joyous time for many reasons—such as vacations and travel, the growth of nature's beauty, and for many, a time for spiritual growth—the end of the summer signifies change. For children and parents, they think the first day of school is the end of the summer, yet other people think of Labor Day as the end of summer. Certainly, in most places around the globe, the end of summer brings cooler temperatures and a change in outdoor activities.

Endless

Often, my thoughts turn to
how the summer felt
when in my childhood.

A child full of wonder,
finishing the school year,
loving to start
what felt like an endless summer.

Where there was nothing we had to do
except play baseball, army, superheroes,
run through the sprinkler or go swimming.

We continued doing these
day in and day out,
until it was all over,
having to wait
for Saturdays and Sundays
to play football in the autumn leaves.

The endless summer came to an end
on Labor Day—
the last day of summer.
Signifying the end of personal freedom,
the end to no expectations,
the end of an endless summer.

The Migrating Snowy Owl

Snowy owls are amazing, beautiful birds loved by many people. For most of the calendar year, snowy owls live in the tundra of the Arctic regions where they breed, including coastal Alaska, Canada, and Greenland. They can also be found in northern Scandinavia, Russia, and northern Siberia. When the winter ices over their normal feeding areas and their food sources become scarce, many will migrate south to less frigid conditions. They seem to like the northeast coast of the United States, including the shores of Long Island, New York. Depending on the weather conditions, they arrive sometime in December and depart for their return home, usually in March as the weather begins to warm up.

Snowy owls can grow to twenty-eight inches in length and weigh three-and-a-quarter to six-and-a-half pounds. They can have a wingspan of forty-nine to fifty-four inches. Female snowys are larger than males and have more darker markings on their feathers. Male snowy owls are mostly all white.

On both their breeding and wintering grounds, their diet can range widely to include small mammals such as lemmings, rodents, rabbits, hares, squirrels, weasels, wading birds, ducks, and geese. They have extraordinary vision and hearing, which is most effective when they hunt. Once the weather warms, they will return to their Arctic homeland.

Majestic Wings

Camouflaged white
in the Arctic tundra,
eating a lemming . . .
or two.

Seeming to be so sweet
in its pure whiteness,
brings terror to its prey.

From November to April,
in the plains of Siberia and the marshlands of Canada,
they are wintering and fly south
to the Canadian-United States border.
Breeding thousands of miles south,
starting in April or May,
egg laying in June,
once a year.

Migration continues
year in and year out.
Flying north,
flying south.
Migration continues,
forever and a day.

Pond Waters

Among the most visited ponds in the United States are Jordan Pond in Acadia National Park, Maine, and Walden Pond in Concord, Massachusetts. Walden Pond is a national landmark as the location where the author Henry David Thoreau lived and wrote some of his famous literary works. But ponds can be found just about everywhere rain falls on a regular basis, or where melting snow ends up in depressions in the ground. A pond is a small body of water, usually smaller than a lake, and it can be part of a wetland area with a variety of aquatic plants and animals.

Ponds usually cover no more than a few acres of land. However, there is no rule to indicate how big a pond can be. Some ponds are also small lakes, and there are ponds created by reservoir overflow. There are also man-made ponds in backyards with small waterfalls and others in industrial settings or apartment complexes that include fountains that circulate the waters.

Plants are an important part of a pond ecosystem because they contribute food and shelter for animals, as well as provide oxygen to the environment through photosynthesis. Many animals without backbones (invertebrates) make their homes in ponds. Some of them spend only part of their life cycles in the water, leaving it once they become adults. There are many types of mammals, birds, fish, and amphibians that live in pond habitats such as frogs and toads. Ponds are a common source of drinking water for many animals that live in nearby forests or wetland areas.

Ripples

Walking the forest floor,
through the trees,
into a gully,
arriving at a pond:
a flock of ducks waddling and quacking.

There is the need
for a calming influence.
As each rock thrown in the pond
reverberates
to see the ripples travel on an endless path,
always followed by
another ripple.

Ripples spread out and disappear in intensity,
overlapping the ripple patterns showing through the pond waters.
I sit down on the rocks by the pond,
thinking intently about my life.

That is what is needed,
an endless stream of ripples
showing me that
"sadness and happiness" both can be an endless destination.
So, happiness must be dropped into the pond,
letting it ripple endlessly.

Rabbits

Rabbits, also known as bunnies or bunny rabbits, live in the wild or are domesticated animals. There are twenty-nine rabbit species and at least 305 breeds of domestic rabbits around the world. More than half of the world's rabbits live in North America, but bunnies are also native to southwest Europe, Sumatra, Southeast Asia, some parts of Japan, and in parts of Africa and South America. The rabbit's appearance is that of an animal that sits on its large hind legs and has shorter front legs. The animal also has large ears that vary in size based on the type.

The eastern cottontail is the most common rabbit species in North America. You'll find them in open parklands, woodland areas, and backyards of homes that have grassy areas, shrubs, woody debris, and trees. The cottontail's diet is all vegetarian, including lawn grasses, clover, crabgrass, dandelions, twigs, bark, flowers, and leaves. They can grow to a length of fourteen to nineteen inches and weigh from one-and-a-half to four-and-a-half pounds.

If chased, the cottontail runs and jumps in a zig-zag pattern, running up to eighteen miles per hour. Oddly enough, when a rabbit first senses danger, it often freezes in place, believing that if it is not moving, it can't be seen. They live in large groups in underground tunnels called warrens with anything from a few to dozens of roommates. A group of rabbits is known as a colony or nest.

The rabbit as a trickster is a part of American popular culture. Probably the best-known rabbit in America is Bugs Bunny, the cartoon character found in animated TV shows and movies from Warner Bros. In many parts of the world, a rabbit's foot is sometimes carried as an amulet believed to bring protection and good luck.

Hippity Hop

Hippity Hop through my garden at my home
on the south shore of Long Island.
My mini lop and mini rex from Germany and France
had outdoor endurance
for the special cage complex they needed to survive and
were the perfect pets for my wife and me plus the kids
and kept my home clean.

Hippity Hop,
through the gardens and over all the continents in the world,
even the Arctic.
So popular is the rabbit that
countries and cultures have claimed its meanings:
fertility, trickster, celestial animal, moon creature, cowardice,
moon creature making rice cakes, deity creating the world,
peace and tranquility.

Popular culture as:
Brer Rabbit, White Rabbit in *Alice in Wonderland*, Bugs Bunny,
Peter Rabbit, rabbit's foot, and "the rabbit died."

Unbeknownst to me some 30+ years later
would my mini lop and mini rex
represent life and beauty itself
as my children grew into adults
and my wife and I were seeking hope
in everyday trials and tribulations.

Rainbows

One of the most well-known songs that describes rainbows and the emotions they create in people is "Somewhere Over the Rainbow," sung by Judy Garland for the 1939 movie *The Wizard of Oz*, followed in popularity by "What a Wonderful World," recorded in 1967 by Louis Armstrong. Judy Garland sang, "Somewhere over the rainbow skies are blue and the dreams that you dare to dream really do come true." And Armstrong sang, "The colors of the rainbow so pretty in the sky are also on the faces of people going by."

There are twelve types of rainbows found around the world. The brightest and most common type of rainbow is called a primary rainbow. Rainbows can be full circles. However, the observer normally sees only an arc formed by illuminated droplets above the ground and centered on a line from the sun to the observer's eye.

The sighting of a rainbow usually brings feelings of awe, excitement, peace, and joy, as well as magic. For many people, they are a sign of hope, the beauty after the storm, and can be seen as a pot of gold and good fortune at the rainbow's end. Because rainbows have several colors, they are considered a type of color symbolism when a person or a culture assign meaning to different colors. During Pride Month, it is not uncommon to see the rainbow flag being proudly displayed as a symbol of the LGBTQ+ rights movement.

Hope

Biblical proportions
in an actual circular shape
where we know rainbows
as half domes.

Light hitting water droplets,
always at that forty-two-degree angle,
and unapproachable from afar.

Children know rainbows
as primary colors and "Roy G. Biv."

Adults know rainbows, Biblical rainbows,
God's promise,
no more destruction by flood,
but what about other means?

Adults know rainbows,
diversity and
what's at the end of a rainbow?
A pot of gold in the old Irish tradition.
Peace after a storm.

What's at the end of a rainbow?
Hope for the future.

Elk

Elk are one of the largest species within the deer family and one of the largest terrestrial mammals living in its native range of North America and Central and East Asia. Adult male elk, referred to as bulls, can weigh between 600 and 1,100 pounds and female elk, known as cows, weigh between 450 and 600 pounds. Elk are light brown with dark brown shaggy manes, especially in winter.

Elk were once found across much of North America, but they were killed off and driven to take refuge in more remote locations. Today they live primarily in western North America, especially in mountainous landscapes such as Colorado's Rocky Mountains, Wyoming's National Elk Refuge, and Yellowstone National Park. Elk live in a variety of habitats, including forests, meadows, and mountains. Their diet includes grasses, tree leaves, twigs, and shrubs. Bark, pine needles, and tree lichens are also eaten in smaller quantities. During the winter months in the snow-covered mountain areas, elk will move to the lower elevations where they can graze.

Like a Reindeer

Grazing on the plains for 25 million years.
10 million strong,
only 1 million left
in North America
in 26 states.

In the deer family,
showing their antlers
to fight over a mate
reminds me of a reindeer.

Reindeer remind me of Christmas
many years ago,
and even now Christmastime
with my family,
with my grandchildren,
the sweet legacy of my children
who I find it hard to remember
when they were the same age as my grandchildren.

My mind finishes wandering,
and my focus is on the elk,
who have been here for 25 million years.
The elk are in a duel,
antlers connected, fighting over a mate,
so, they continue their legacy.

Forests and Woods

The terms forests and woods (woodland) define similar but different areas of trees. The main difference is the density (how close trees grow) and the size of the area they grow in. A tight growth of trees in a forest creates a dense canopy limiting the sunlight that filters to the ground. Woods, on the other hand, have more space between trees and therefore a less dense canopy. There are three general types of forest that exist: temperate, tropical, and boreal. Experts estimate that these forests cover approximately one-third of Earth's surface. Temperate forests are found across eastern North America and Eurasia.

No matter what you call them, these wooded areas are critical to our planet's health. The trees that populate our forests and woods do so much. They clean the air, mitigate climate change, and provide habitat for millions of wildlife species. In addition, there are many positive health benefits when people spend time in nature's woodland areas. Some of the most interesting evidence of the health benefits of nature is coming out of Japan and revolves around the popular practice of *Shinrin-yoku* or "forest bathing." Studies in the last few years show forest bathing is also increasing a component of the immune system that fights cancer. Research indicates forest bathing also provides a defense against the pangs of anxiety, stress, depression, and other inflictions on one's mind.

A Great Tree

Deep in the forests and woods,
there is a clearing
where the leaves have fallen,
landing on branches
strewn around by the wind.

Deep in the forests and woods,
there is a favorite tree,
once a baby tree
where my son and I
always went
in the springtime many years ago.
We climbed the branches
and hid in its tree hollow.

As the years went by
the baby tree became a great tree
towering over the undergrowth.

If one could see inside the tree trunk,
the rings of age in the great tree
stand guard through history,
covering land that has been there
over the centuries.

Deep in the forests and woods,
there is the owl
perched on a tree,
the favorite tree
where my son and I
continued to always go.

Years went by
and the favorite tree
became a great tree
where some other father and son
visited from time to time
creating new memories.

Frogs

There are over 6,000 species of frogs worldwide—109 species in the United States and ten found in New York state. Frogs develop in stages beginning with the egg stage and then hatching as tadpoles and morphing into frogs as they grow. They have excellent night vision and are very sensitive to movement. The bulging eyes of most frogs allow them to see in front, to the sides, and partially behind them.

Frogs eat untold billions of insects each year, making them economically valuable to agriculture. They also provide a critical food source for birds, fish, snakes, and other wildlife. But the most important contribution frogs make may be their role as environmental indicators. When pollution or other environmental changes affect a habitat, frogs are often the first casualties. These delicate creatures provide an early warning for endangered ecosystems.

Ribbit

Jumping after flies,
croaking for a mate,
louder than heard by another creature,
some very odd anatomy,
and some species can kill 100,000 people
with the use of 1 ounce of their produced toxin.

Frogs kissed,
turned into princes.
frogs in plagues in Egypt.
frogs in movies.
frogs as Muppets.

Thousands of species.
Some small.
Some large.
Some called toads.
Some translucent.
Some bland.
Some colorful.

Frogs were dissected in biology class
until animal welfare laws.
Toads still alive at the Trinity Site in Los Alamos.
Frogs used in medical experiments,
for fertility,
but deformed frogs are seen in rivers around the world.
Giving us reason to believe
we are slowly killing the environment.

Raccoons

Like the deer population, people either enjoy watching them or hate them because they eat or damage landscapes and vegetable gardens. Children especially find them cute because of their masked faces and black-ringed bushy tails. Adult raccoons can grow to sixteen to twenty-eight inches and can weigh seven to twenty pounds. Being nocturnal, they are more active and feed at night.

There are seven raccoon species that live in North and South America. The most common and well-known is the North American raccoon, which ranges from northern Canada and most of the United States southward into South America. They are a medium-sized mammal native to North America. Raccoons can adapt to many living environments, including farms, country homes, and city areas. In woodland locations, raccoons eat birds, insects, fruits, nuts, and seeds. In residential areas, they will knock over garbage cans seeking food and will locate pet food if left outside. If they live near waterways, raccoons will include fish in their diets.

Rocket

Discovered by Christopher Columbus
on the island of Hispaniola,
the raccoon, or racoon,
or mapache as the Aztecs knew them.

Their hands are their most useful tool
to eat fish, worms, plants, insects,
and sometimes small birds.
Mapache is a hand washer,
and the racoon "douses" their food
before eating.

Interesting to look at
but not well-liked.
Stealing from garbage cans,
spilling refuse about,
their face colored by a mask,
begging for food.

Some fast facts:
having natural spirit powers,
known as a trickster, Davy Crockett's hat;
and a famous character in a movie—
Rocket from *Guardians of the Galaxy.*

The Heron Family

There are seventy-two identified species of herons around the world, some of which are called bitterns and egrets. On Long Island, New York, the common herons found near the waters include the great blue heron, the black-crowned night heron, the yellow-crowned night heron, and the green heron. The night herons are named because while they do hunt during the day, they do most of their hunting for food at night. The great blue herons are the largest bird in the heron family, growing up to four feet tall with a six to seven-foot wingspan. Watching a great blue heron spread their wings and fly, these large birds are said to have a prehistoric look. While associated with water since their diet consists of mainly fish and crustaceans, herons are actually non-swimming birds that wade the shorelines.

Herons have an interesting fishing method. They stand motionless for long periods in shallow water, watching and waiting for their prey. They catch small fish with a quick thrust of their bills into the water. Herons will swallow fish and small crustaceans whole. Their feeding habits are fun to watch if you have the patience to observe them.

While herons as a species have a relatively low conservation concern, threats include draining and development of wetland habitat, and reduced water quality due to contaminated runoff. They are susceptible to pollutants such as persistent organochlorine pesticides, PCBs, and heavy metals.

The Archaeopteryx

I had the patience,
the other day,
to observe
the heron feed.

Watching its prey,
diving headfirst,
swallowing the fish whole.
Then, flying off to the next prey.

Reminiscent of the ancient one,
the archaeopteryx.
Majestic as it takes flight,
we can see why, in Buddhism,
the heron is purity, transformation, and wisdom.

Taking flight to find its prey,
we are reminded that in Native American culture
the heron is renewal, rejuvenation, and rebirth—
part of a larger cycle of life and death.

Photo by Kieran O'Keefe

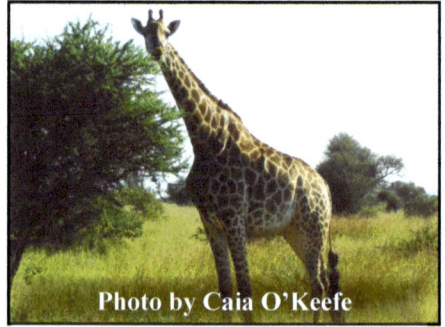

Photo by Caia O'Keefe

Photo by Caitlyn O'Keefe

Photo by Kieran O'Keefe

Big Game Wildlife

When writing a book about nature, one can't leave out the subject of "big game." For many experts on wildlife, a big game land animal is any animal over forty pounds. So, moose, elk, and deer would be considered big game. The type of big game land animals referred to in this section are the wonderous animals found in Africa. These include elephants, lions, leopards, and giraffes to name a few. They are truly amazing in terms of size, survival, and special features like speed when hunting for food. The four photos above were all taken on safari in South Africa.

The African elephant is the largest land animal in the world. It can range in size from nineteen to twenty-four feet in length and weigh from 13,000 to 19,000 pounds. They feed on mostly shrubbery, vines, herbs, and tree leaves. African elephants live from sixty to seventy years of age. African giraffes are very fast animals. At a gallop, they can reach speeds of nearly forty miles per hour. They are also the tallest animals in the world and feed on leaves, flowers, fruits, and shoots of woody plants. Male giraffes can grow to sixteen to eighteen feet tall and weigh up to 4,200 pounds; females are fourteen to sixteen feet tall and weigh up to 2,600 pounds. Giraffes have an artistic look: their coat has a pattern of brown patches against a white background.

Lions are Africa's largest carnivores. Males can weigh up to 575 pounds and female lions up to 280 pounds. The male African leopard can grow to 130 pounds and the females from 77 to 88 pounds. When on the run, leopards can reach speeds of sixty miles per hour.

Big Game on the African Plains

Elephants, hippos, rhinos, and giraffes:
big game on the African Plains.

Mastodons and mammoths roamed the Earth a million years ago
grazing on the African Plains,
descendants of the largest land animal,
the elephant.
Roaming in herds, honoring their dead,
represents rainbows in Hinduism,
and hunted for their tusks.

Anthracotheres diverged from whales millions of years ago,
and the hippo became semiaquatic with webbed feet.
They defecate in water claiming territory,
represent the Egyptian god Set,
and hunted for their meat.

Paracerath roaming 14 million years ago
became the rhino.
Legends have them putting out fires,
represent the vehicle for the Hindu god Agni,
and hunted for their horns.

Climacoceras grazing 15 million years ago
became the giraffe.
The largest hoofed animals, they fight by "necking,"
represent the arrival of a sage,
and hunted for their tails.

Elephants, hippos, rhinos, and giraffes:
big game on the African Plains—
majestic and vulnerable,

Slowly they reach extinction.

Photo by Kieran O'Keefe

Photo by Caitlyn O'Keefe

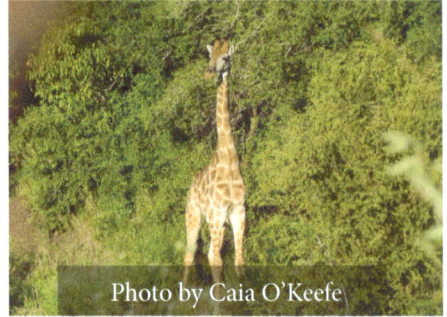
Photo by Caia O'Keefe

Big Game Kids

Of the opening music found in New York City Broadway plays, none are more recognized than the lyrics from *The Lion King*: "From the time we arrive on the planet, and, blinking, step into the sun . . . It's the circle of life."

Of all the wonderous aspects of nature, none is more amazing than reproduction. And with big game wildlife, it gets even more astonishing. To see elephants, the largest land animal on Earth, be so attentive to their young, or to observe lions, the fiercest of all, be so affectionate to their offspring takes your breath away. On average, newborn elephant calves stand about three feet high and weigh 264 pounds at birth. The newborn is helped to its feet by its mother and other females. Lion cubs weigh only about four pounds at birth, which is so much smaller than the 400 pounds they can reach when they grow up. At birth, giraffe calves are about six feet tall and weigh between 100 to 150 pounds.

While we are looking at the beginning of life for animals, what better time to discuss a gigantic problem? All around the globe, nature is in trouble. The effects of climate change, land development, poaching, and pollution are shrinking our wildlife populations and our forest environments. The World Wildlife Fund estimates that "African elephant populations have declined by 62% between 2002-2011 and they have lost 30% of their geographical range." With an estimated 20,000 lions remaining, their population continues to shrink rapidly and is expected to suffer an additional 50% decline in the next two decades. And it is the same problem for white rhinos, Grevy's zebras, and mountain gorillas—they are at risk of becoming extinct. As you spend more time in nature, learn what you can do to make a difference in the world.

Kids on the African Plains

Elephants, hippos, rhinos, and giraffes:
big game and their young, on the African Plains,
still vulnerable to extinction.

Mastodons and mammoths roamed the Earth a million years ago
grazing on the African Plains,
descendants of the largest land animal,
the elephant.
Pregnant for 18 to 24 months, mother's care up to 4 years.
Still hunted for their tusks as they age.

Anthracotheres diverged from whales millions of years ago,
and the hippo became semiaquatic with webbed feet.
Pregnant for 8 months, mother's care for 3 to 7 years.
Still hunted for their meat as they age.

Paraceratherium roaming 14 million years ago
became the rhino.
Pregnant for 14 to 18 months except in captivity,
mother's care for one calf at a time.
Still hunted for their horns as they age.

Climacoceras grazing 15 million years ago
became the giraffe.
Pregnant for 18 months, mother's care for 14 months.
Still hunted for their tails as they age.

Elephants, hippos, rhinos, and giraffes:
big game on the African Plains,
having babies on the African Plains—
majestic and vulnerable;

Slowly they will also reach extinction.

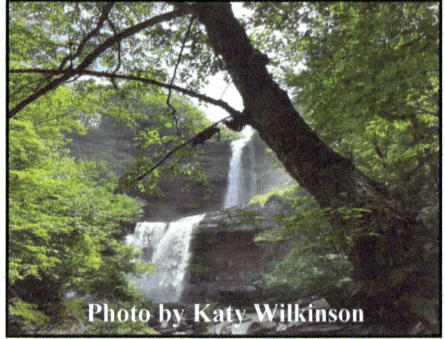

Photo by Katy Wilkinson

Waterfalls

Of the *natural wonders of the world*, Victoria Waterfalls and Niagara Falls make the list. They keep company with the Grand Canyon, Mount Everest, and Great Barrier Reef to name a few others. Why? Because seeing two of the largest walls of water forming a curtain is stunning. About 1 million people visit Victoria Falls and 20 million visit Niagara each year, ranking them among the most popular tourist's spots in the world. Victoria is about 355 feet high and 5,604 feet wide. Its combined dimensions make it the largest waterfall surface. Niagara is 176 feet high and is shared by two countries, the United States and Canada.

There are 7,800 waterfalls documented around the world. In general, people love them. The combined sounds and impressive visuals almost always make people smile. They also make great photographic subjects because of the challenge of composing an image that is suitable, and because photographers can change their shutter settings to either freeze the droplets of water in place or smooth out the droplets to create a milky look to the water in the photo.

Due to the effects of climate change, extreme weather changes have threatened Victoria Falls (bottom right). In May of 2021 (bottom left), a drought so severe the Zambezi River, which feeds the Falls, dried up the water flowing over the Falls, giving it an eerie, unbelievable look. The Zambezi was reduced to a relative trickle and Victoria Falls temporarily ran dry.

A Million Years

Traveling by train
miles and miles and miles away.
Taking vintage train cars
hours and hours and hours,
over the green mountain hills,
across the flat green plains
of farmland,
finally stopping at a station no longer needed.

Walking along a dirt road no longer used,
to the path
seen only in my dreams,
arriving at a waterfall.

Flowing down from one river to another,
the white-water raft abandoned some years ago
is up against the rocks in the river.
Tracing the path back to the waterfall,
viewing the constant flow
that has gone on and on, for hours,
days, weeks, months, years, decades, centuries.

As I stare at the water flowing
that goes on and on for hours,
for the time staying here
before my train trip back home,
again realizing that the waterfall has been flowing
on and on, for hours,
days, weeks, months, years, decades, centuries . . .
a million years.

Songbirds

On any spring morning, hiking along a woodland path, you might hear the singing of a songbird. A songbird is a bird that produces musical sounds which are like singing. Male songbirds do most of the singing to attract a mate or defend its territory. There are over 5,000 species of songbirds in the world.

Over fifty species of songbirds call Long Island, New York home. Some just pass through during migrations; others make Long Island their permanent home. Each species has specific dietary needs, as well as different habitat requirements and nesting habits. The photos above are representative of the songbirds found on Long Island. Clockwise from the upper left, the American robin, northern cardinal, Baltimore oriole, and the magnificent scarlet tanager are four of the most common songbirds.

What gives the songbird the ability to sing is an amazing science. They have precise control over a specialized vocal organ called a syrinx. While almost all birds use a syrinx to produce sound, songbirds also have a complex set of muscles attached to the syrinx that gives them greater control, and as a result, songbirds can produce the most dramatic ballads.

The Countertenor

Songbirds are, for a word, natural.
Amazing in their vocal range
the voice box structure
begs a question: How could it be?

There are Streisand and Sinatra, and Bennett and Bublé,
and there is Countertenor Andreas Scholl,
having the range of a songbird.

Hundreds of bird species,
hundreds of bird calls.
Hundreds of bird species,
hundreds of ways to communicate.
Hundreds of bird species in hundreds of locales,
but only
the songbirds sing.

How did it happen?
How did the songbird find its voice?
It could only be
divine intervention.

Autumn Colors

In general, most people around the world love to see the magnificent colors of the trees once the cooler weather brings change. During this time, the leaves on trees that were once green explode into beautiful shades of red, gold, yellow, and orange. The colors are especially breathtaking in places like New England in the United States, the Douro River Valley in Portugal, and Bavaria in Germany, inspiring many people to travel to these spots to take in the scenery.

Trees that have leaves that change color in fall are deciduous. (Evergreen trees with needles do not change colors and are coniferous.) Deciduous trees usually have large, broad leaves. Most of the year, these leaves are green because of the chlorophyll they use to absorb energy from sunlight during photosynthesis. The leaves convert the energy into sugars to feed the tree. As the season changes, temperatures drop and days get shorter. Trees get less direct sunlight, and the chlorophyll in the leaves breaks down.

There are many theories as to why people love to see the fall scenery of autumn color. Some psychologists explain that a person's childhood memories of fall foliage trigger happy thoughts. Others explain there is a natural high associated with the scenery experience and to the uplifting inspiration that follows.

On the Overlook

Driving up Route 104
in Cayuga County,
there are rolling hills on the horizon.
Along the parkway there are rocks and boulders
lining the high country.

As the road winds around and around,
there are the maple and oak trees
shading the roadway
along the way.

It is apparent,
its autumn upstate
where the coolness permeates the air.
Its crispness invigorates me.

Stopping along the way,
it is best to go by the overlook
to snap my photos of wildlife and the beautiful autumn colors
of the maple and oak trees lining
Route 104 in Cayuga County.

When thinking, after the photos are snapped,
it's important to remember that:
carotenoids, chlorophyll, coevolution, are:
Red, orange, brown, yellow—
autumn colors to you and me.

Photo by Paul Mila

Magnificent Whales

Amazingly, there are ninety species of whales found in ocean waters around the world. The largest whale, the blue whale, can grow to be 100 feet long, weighing up to 200 tons. That's as much as thirty-three elephants. The smallest whale on Earth is the dwarf sperm whale. It can measure up to nine feet long, weighing between 400 and 600 hundred pounds. The blue whale is not only the biggest whale living today, but the biggest creature ever to have lived on Earth. They are mind-bogglingly gigantic—much larger than any of the dinosaurs.

The humpback whale pictured above is among the largest whales. It can grow to forty-nine feet long and weigh forty-four tons. The humpback whale is a popular whale for whale watchers because it is known for breaching the water's surface and seemingly performing aerial maneuvers as it blows streams of water from its blowhole. Whales are unique, beautiful, graceful, and mysterious; they nurture, form friendships, innovate, grieve, play, sing, and cooperate with one another.

Even though whales live in the water, like humans they breathe air and are warm-blooded mammals who also nurse their young. Interestingly, humpback whales give birth to live young and feed their young milk.

Unfortunately, the whale's large size and mythical aura does not protect them; six out of the thirteen great whale species are classified as endangered or vulnerable, even after decades of protection. An estimated minimum of 300,000 whales and dolphins are killed each year because of fisheries' bycatch, while others succumb to a myriad of threats, including shipping and habitat loss. This photo was taken about eighty miles north of the Dominican Republic in an area known as Silver Banks. It is protected by NOAA as the "Sanctuary for the Marine Mammals of the Dominican Republic."

There She Blows

Amazing, majestic animal in the sea,
a mammal no less.
48 million years ago
land dwelling into the sea.
Little known genealogy,
hippopotamus is a relative.

Nostrils
are a blowhole.
Live birth at sea.
Blubber for food,
oil for light and heat.
Centuries hunting them toward extinction.

Bible stories abound.
Genesis, Jonah, and Job.
In the Quran.
In Buddhism.
In Viking and Norse lore.

Whale watching,
conservational programs worldwide,
credited with saving the whale
so their majestic splendor goes on,
hopefully, for centuries to come.

Photo by Jeanne Cardone

Photo by Jeanne Cardone

Our Loveable Pets

There is no question that from companionship to emotional support, pets are a vital part of their owners' lives. From this give-and-take relationship, pets receive the care they need and tons of affection, and people receive what they need most—unconditional love.

Research studies have shown that interactions between owners and their pets can reduce stress, lower blood pressure, and without a doubt, add to a person's happiness. So much so that the majority of pet owners consider their pets to be part of their family. As of 2023, 66% of U.S. households (86.9 million homes) own a pet. The most common pets in the United States are dogs, followed a close second by cats. After that, there's still a lot of love for other animals. Millions of households include tropical fish, birds, small animals such as hamsters and rabbits, and an occasional bearded dragon.

Some years back, I observed an amazing therapy dog visit to residents in a nursing home in New York City. At first, the residents were seen as depressed, lonely, and unresponsive. Then, the dogs showed up and the change was unforgettable. It started with giant smiles, animated arms, even shouts of joy.

The love of a dog, say a golden retriever's feelings for its owner, can be observed in the greeting the dog gives when an owner returns to the home—even just for a few minutes to retrieve the mail. Its tail wagging and movement that excites will make anyone smile in response.

The Family Dogs and Cats

As a young boy,
having a dog that would be my buddy, and other animals,
was a dream.

My dream of a dog, and another dog, and a cat, and another cat
had to wait until my own family was a reality,
and when we did get a dog, I called him "buddy."

When we had 3 children in 12 years, and then after 5 more years,
my children and wife thought the family unit would not be complete
until we had a dog, and another dog, and a cat, and another cat.

The buddy dog was the leader of the pack,
watching over the other dog, the cat, and the other cat
and watching over all of us in his protective, circling, herding way.

The buddy dog is not well now, but one thing remains:
When finally my dream was realized;
the buddy dog completed our family unit,
along with the 3 kids, the other dog, the cat, the other cat,
and the heart and soul of the family, my wife.

Somehow, she knew that the more love in the home, the better
to help us get over pain and heartache, or even everyday issues.

AFTERWORD
by John P. Cardone

Reviewing the contents of our book, *The Poetry & Wonders of Nature*—seeing the photographs, reading the subject descriptions, and understanding Jeff Rimland's emotional connections to nature in his poetry—I find myself thinking about three very important messages for our readers and for our readers to spread the word with their social media platforms. The first is that the beauty and wonder of nature could very well be lost to future generations. It has been reported on global news channels and written in magazines, newspapers, and scientific journals. The World Wildlife Fund states, "Sea levels are rising, and oceans are becoming warmer. Longer, more intense droughts threaten crops, wildlife, and freshwater supplies. From polar bears in the Arctic to marine turtles off the coast of Africa, our planet's diversity of life is at risk from the changing climate."

The challenge of correcting climate change and stopping deforestation is huge. Some say it is too late. But no, what choice do we have? If you are not involved, change things up and become involved. Look into how you can support the environmental organizations around the world (many are seen in the "References and Resources" section to follow), become members, and offer financial support for their efforts. Then, contact your local and state representatives and let them know you vote for politicians who want to combat climate change. You can make a difference!

Next, learn more about how spending time in nature has a healing power for you—there are physical and mental benefits for every minute. Nature is a perfect place to practice the meditation known as "mindfulness." And again, my book, *The Healing Power of Nature* (details in the "Other Books" section on page 83), cites studies and research that prove the science of this power. Of course, there are mentions of my firsthand experiences describing how my cancer fights were helped by time in nature. This includes health stress reduction, lower blood pressure, and improved physical and mental health.

Lastly, there is a heartfelt tug regarding the importance of educating our children and grandchildren—to prepare them to be better stewards of their future world. Children are nature sponges and enjoy seeing the natural beauty around them and the wildlife that live in these environments. Do online searches for the places to visit and make it a habit to get out. If the weather is not favorable, or poor health prevents an outing, books and websites can bring nature experiences right to your computer. The one thing you'll see are the smiles on the children's faces. They really do love nature—you just have to make it happen.

DESCRIPTION REFERENCES AND RESOURCES

www.britannica.com/science/wave-water

www.mywavefinder.com/2019/10/16/10-biggest-waves-in-the-world/

https://en.wikipedia.org/wiki/Wind_wave

https://a-z-animals.com/blog/bald-eagle-population-by-state/#:~:text=There%20are%20an%20estimated%20316%2C700,and%20Wildlife%20Service%20(USFWS)

https://senecaparkzoo.org/bald-eagle/?gclid=Cj0KCQjwqoibBhDUARIsAH2OpWhrUsrPmJVwH6TjLqiHeSXAtqZgz7tQqJFMgQHZ2-o7FU1677u4SnAaArhgEALw_wcB

www.hummingbirdcentral.com/hummingbird-migration-spring-2022-map.htm

www.perkypet.com/advice/bird-watching/hummingbird-migration/migration-facts#:~:text=Each%20year%2C%20thousands%20of%20Ruby,miles%20to%20reach%20U.S.%20shores.

https://wildlife.org/hummingbirds-have-flight-range-of-over-1000-miles/

https://en.wikipedia.org/wiki/White-tailed_deer

https://en.wikipedia.org/wiki/List_of_snowiest_places_in_the_United_States_by_state

www.mercurynews.com/2018/10/18/photos-famous-snow-covered-peaks-from-around-the-world/#:~:text=Mount%20Everest%20of%20the%20Great,29%2C035%20feet%20(8%2C850%20meters).

www.nps.gov/places/cadillac-mountain.htm

www.allaboutbirds.org/guide/Osprey/overview

https://sageography.co.za/wiki/grade-12-caps/geomorphology/drainage-systems-in-south-africa/types-of-rivers/

https://en.wikipedia.org/wiki/Monarch_butterfly

https://en.wikipedia.org/wiki/Woodpecker#:~:text=Woodpeckers%20are%20diurnal%2C%20roosting%20at,distinct%20from%20its%20nesting%20site.

https://en.wikipedia.org/wiki/Mute_Swan

DESCRIPTION REFERENCES AND RESOURCES (con't)

Mute Swan Overview, All About Birds, Cornell Lab of Ornithology

www.trumpeterswansociety.org/swan-information/faqs.html

https://www.allaboutbirds.org/guide/Canada_Goose/id

https://www.maritimeaquarium.org/meet-the-animals?gclid=CjwKCAi
ApvebBhAvEiwAe7mHSBzSd07DDAbLX5Gdq1z2H3aCiHLZX1RRKo
Yxy3P7rRwbxnF7M_mT8hoCtGEQAvD_BwE#item=402554

https://en.wikipedia.org/wiki/Insect

https://www.humanesociety.org/animals/insects

www.nationalgeographic.com/animals/mammals/facts/
chipmunks#:~:text=Size%20relative%20to%20a%20teacup,of%20
starring%20roles%20in%20Hollywood

https://animalcorner.org/animals/chipmunk/

https://en.wikipedia.org/wiki/Alvin_and_the_
Chipmunks#:~:text=The%20group%20consists%20of%20
three,%2C%20David%20%22Dave%22%20Seville

https://www.kpcnews.com/columnists/neil_case/kpcnews/
article_11f43554-a3d6-5a92-9d56-d8eba974f28c.html

https://lpatucson.org/south/why-summer-ends-and-autumn-begins-
this-month/#:~:text=Scientifically%2C%20however%2C%20summer

https://www.nbcnews.com/sciencemain/what-defines-end-summer-its-
just-how-our-planet-tilted-4b11221602

https://senecaparkzoo.org/snowy-owl/?gclid=Cj0KCQjw7uSkBhDGAR
IsAMCZNJvWI65FRlqf1MnaWb6XDcg4LDTc7PlBlDrMawkQXaLy2s
xqcmmAzUQaAr1YEALw_wcB

https://www.allaboutbirds.org/guide/Snowy_Owl/id?gclid=Cj0KCQjw
7uSkBhDGARIsAMCZNJspaJOW1vwVoAingKRrLy_6BZBGsv0Dh9G
kZv_19pV4D7n_GV3QF1YaAuBWEALw_wcB

https://www.allaboutbirds.org/guide/Snowy_Owl/lifehistory

https://en.wikipedia.org/wiki/Pond

http://worldlandforms.com/landforms/pond/

https://kids.britannica.com/students/article/pond-life/605107

DESCRIPTION REFERENCES AND RESOURCES (con't)

https://en.wikipedia.org/wiki/Rabbit

https://a-z-animals.com/animals/rabbit/

https://en.wikipedia.org/wiki/Rainbow

https://www.worldatlas.com/articles/what-are-the-different-types-of-rainbows.html#:~:text=Primary%20rainbows%20are%20also%20known,known%20as%20higher%2Dorder%20rainbows.

https://en.wikipedia.org/wiki/Elk

https://landpotential.org/habitat-hub/elk/

https://www.fs.usda.gov/detail/npnht/learningcenter/nature-science/?cid=fsbdev3_055714

https://www.worldwildlife.org/initiatives/forests

https://ucmp.berkeley.edu/exhibits/biomes/forests.php

What's the difference?: Woods vs. forest | Forest Preserve District of Will County (reconnectwithnature.org)

https://www.reconnectwithnature.org/news-events/the-buzz/what-the-difference-woods-vs-forest/

https://www.britannica.com/story/how-did-the-rainbow-flag-become-a-symbol-of-lgbt-pride

https://www.amnh.org/exhibitions/frogs-a-chorus-of-colors/frogs-and-the-ecosystem/what-are-frogs-worth#:~:text=Frogs%20eat%20untold%20billions%20of,their%20role%20as%20environmental%20indicators.

https://www.longislandaquarium.com/wp-content/uploads/FROGS-and-TOADS-2019-website.pdf

https://www.dec.ny.gov/docs/remediation_hudson_pdf/frogs.pdf

https://www.dec.ny.gov/animals/9358.html

https://www.britannica.com/animal/raccoon#ref56676

https://www.allaboutbirds.org/guide/Black-crowned_Night-Heron/overview#

https://www.allaboutbirds.org/guide/Great_Blue_Heron/overview

DESCRIPTION REFERENCES AND RESOURCES (con't)

https://en.wikipedia.org/wiki/Heron

https://www.allaboutbirds.org/guide/Yellow-crowned_Night-Heron/overview

https://en.wikipedia.org/wiki/List_of_heaviest_land_mammals

https://www.pittsburghzoo.org/Animal-African-Elephant

https://lionrecoveryfund.org/biology-behavior/

https://animalia.bio/south-african-giraffe

https://www.denverzoo.org/wp-content/uploads/2018/09/Reticulated-Giraffe.pdf

https://www.scienceabc.com/humans/are-artists-wired-differently-than-non-artists.

https://sdzwildlifeexplorers.org/stories/learning-be-lions#:~:text=Tiny%20lion%20cubs%20will%20grow,reach%20when%20they%20grow%20up!html#:~:text=There%20is%20a%20difference%20in,that%20non%2Dartists%20would%20miss.

https://www.jakeyou.com/blog/the-artist-mindset-how-to-think-like-an-artist#:~:text=Put%20simply%2C%20the%20artist%20mindset,ability%20to%20draw%20unique%20conclusions

https://seaworld.org/animals/all-about/elephants/care-of-young/#:~:text=Calves%20at%20Birth, at%20birth.

https:// https://www.geographyrealm.com/waterfalls-that-flow-into-the-ocean/#:~:text=Out%20of%20the%20over%207%2C800,%2C%20inlet%2C%20or%20fjord).www.awf.org/news/endangered-species-day-saving-mountain-gorillas-african-elephants

https://www.overandaboveafrica.com/lions?gad=1&gclid=Cj0KCQjw8NilBhDOARIsAHzpbLBv8jUtHESOm6sikwJsd2AI0l2W-8GYoeHcjaZgPh8nX2pOSJNFKAUaAobyEALw_wcB

https://7wonders.org/natural-wonders/

https://7wonders.org/africa/zambia/livingstone/victoria-falls/

https://habri.org/pressroom/20200420?gad=1&gclid=CjwKCAjwtuOlBhBREiwA7agf1oGxjFE_YaVf2lVx8b13bcTuN7jaByvsConevW__

DESCRIPTION REFERENCES AND RESOURCES (con't)

https://www.psychologytoday.com/us/blog/relationship-and-trauma-insights/202204/the-3-reasons-we-love-our-pets-so-much#:~:text=Pets%20provide%20the%20non%2Dcomplex,connection%2C%20attunement%2C%20and%20presence.

https://www.psychologytoday.com/us/blog/relationship-and-trauma-insights/202204/the-3-reasons-we-love-our-pets-so-much#:~:text=Pets%20provide%20the%20non%2Dcomplex,connection%2C%20attunement%2C%20and%20presence.

https://www.worldwildlife.org/threats/effects-of-climate-change#:~:text=Sea%20levels%20are%20rising%20and,risk%20from%20the%20changing%20climate

https://www.audubon.org/news/what-songbird-exactly#:~:text=All%20songbirds%20are%20perching%20birds,are%20called%20oscines%2C%20or%20songbirds.

https://www.britannica.com/animal/songbird

https://wildlifecenterli.org/wildlife-information/songbirds/

https://www.worldwildlife.org/species/whale

https://us.whales.org/whales-dolphins/facts-about-whales/

https://www.westernunion.com/blog/en/10-reasons-autumn-one-best-seasons/

https://www.si.edu/stories/why-do-leaves-change-color-fall#:~:text=As%20the%20season%20changes%2C%20temperatures,masked%20during%20the%20warmer%20months.

POETRY REFERENCES AND RESOURCES

https://en.wikipedia.org/wiki/Bald_eagle

https://www.thespruce.com/fun-facts-about-hummingbirds-387106

https://en.wikipedia.org/wiki/Osprey

https://en.wikipedia.org/wiki/Monarch_butterfly

https://en.wikipedia.org/wiki/Woodpecker

https://www.nps.gov/asis/learn/nature/horses.htm

https://en.wikipedia.org/wiki/Mute_swan

https://en.wikipedia.org/wiki/Canada_goose

Cooperative Hunting Behavior of Harbor Seals (Phoca vitulina) in Whatcom Creek Delaney Adams Western Washington University July 1, 2020

https://www.cresli.org/common/news/articles/article_detail.cfm?QID=11251&clientID=12000&topicID=0&subsection=sidebar

https://en.wikipedia.org/wiki/Blue_jay

https://www.britannica.com/animal/social-insect

https://en.wikipedia.org/wiki/Chipmunk

https://www.mentalfloss.com/article/94532/12-beautiful-blooms-bouquet-flower-etymologies

https://en.wikipedia.org/wiki/Turtle

https://en.wikipedia.org/wiki/Snowy_owl

https://en.wikipedia.org/wiki/Rabbit

https://education.nationalgeographic.org/resource/rainbow/

https://en.wikipedia.org/wiki/Elk

https://www.farmersalmanac.com/frog-facts#:~:text=1%20Frogs%20live%20around%20the%20world%2C%20on%20every,up%20to%20a%20mile%20away%21%20...%20More%20items

POETRY REFERENCES AND RESOURCES (CON'T)

https://en.wikipedia.org/wiki/Frog#Call

https://www.wbur.org/hereandnow/2018/07/16/trinity-nuclear-test-toads

https://en.wikipedia.org/wiki/Raccoon

https://en.wikipedia.org/wiki/Heron

https://en.wikipedia.org/wiki/Elephant

https://en.wikipedia.org/wiki/Hippopotamus

https://en.wikipedia.org/wiki/Rhinoceros

https://en.wikipedia.org/wiki/Giraffe

https://en.wikipedia.org/wiki/Elephant

https://en.wikipedia.org/wiki/Hippopotamus

https://animalsresearch.com/hippo-pregnancy/

https://en.wikipedia.org/wiki/Rhinoceros

https://en.wikipedia.org/wiki/Giraffe

https://www.singwise.com/articles/understanding-vocal-range-vocal-registers-and-voice-type-a-glossary-of-vocal-terms#:~:text=Males%20with%20high%20vocal%20ranges,specifically%20referred%20to%20as%20sopranist).
https://youtube.com/watch?v=N7XH-58eB8c&feature=sharea
https://en.wikipedia.org/wiki/Autumn_leaf_color
https://en.wikipedia.org/wiki/Whale
Rimland, J.(2010). Reflections on Half Century. Eloquent Books. P 40

OTHER NON-FICTION BOOKS BY
JOHN P. CARDONE

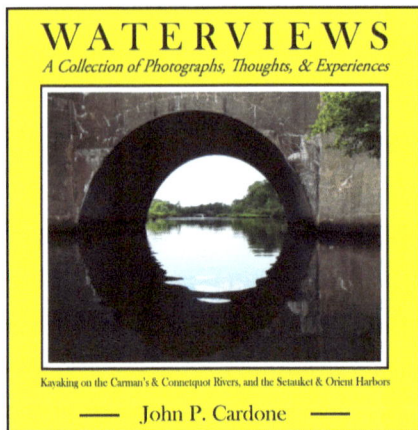

WATERVIEWS
A Collection of Photographs, Thoughts, & Experiences

Kayaking on the Carman's & Connetquot Rivers, and the Setauket & Orient Harbors

—— John P. Cardone ——

Waterviews is a collection of photographs, thoughts, and experiences acquired while kayaking the Carman's and Connetquot Rivers, and the Setauket and Orient Harbors of Long Island, New York. It contains over 75 scenic and wildlife photographs, most snapped from the unique vantage point of a kayak floating on top of the water. Topics include the science of waterway formation, locations and tours of the waters, Long Island history, photography, and information about kayak basics, techniques, and safety. *Waterviews* also explores subjects that surface when out on a paddle, such as happiness, relaxation, sickness, loss, and friendship.

"In Waterviews, Cardone takes us along on an informative and enjoyable excursion into a Long Island that most never see."

John Hanc, Newsday writer on the outdoors and local history

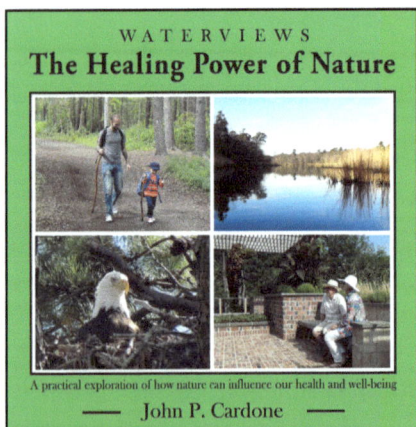

WATERVIEWS
The Healing Power of Nature

A practical exploration of how nature can influence our health and well-being

—— John P. Cardone ——

The Healing Power of Nature is a practical exploration of how spending time with nature can influence our health and well-being. Along the way, John calls on over 40 years as a patient and health education video producer, his own fight with illness, and his years as a lover of the outdoors, while presenting the scientific facts. Learn about which nature we are referring to, the importance of calming your mind, the health benefits of the outdoors, happiness and the restorative advantage of nature, and why it is especially important to share this spirit with children.

"If everyone was required to read Cardone's Healing Power of Nature, the world would be a better and happier place. And I think our health insurance costs would be a lot lower as well."

Sal Randazzo, Retired Educator

OTHER NON-FICTION BOOKS BY
JOHN P. CARDONE

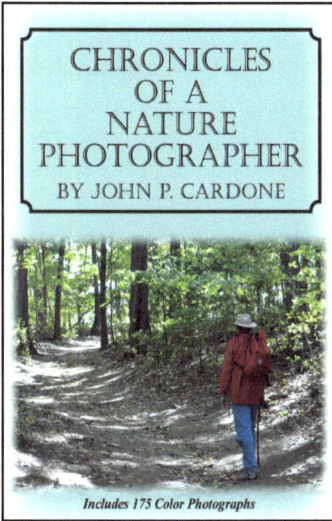

CHRONICLES
OF A
NATURE
PHOTOGRAPHER
BY JOHN P. CARDONE

Includes 175 Color Photographs

Written to entertain and inform, *Chronicles of a Nature Photographer* consists of 140 pages, 15 chapters, 175 color photographs, and countless nature stories in a series of personal essays. In *Chronicles*, John brings the reader on a journey of nature sightings through his first-hand experiences illustrated by his wonderful nature photographs. Along the way, he provides photography techniques and tips for different outdoor settings, sometimes while hiking and sometimes while kayaking the waters. Be inspired as you read about how John's fight with cancer was helped by hummingbirds, how observing ospreys can be a mindful experience, what it means to search for snowy owls and wild horses, or feeling a higher power while snowshoeing the Rocky Mountains, plus much more. If you like the outdoors or enjoy nature photographs, then you will be captivated by the stories within this book. In *Chronicles of a Nature Photographer,* there is something for everyone to enjoy.

"Contains great information about the natural history of many species and their habitats."
Marisa Nelson, Assistant Director, Quogue Wildlife Refuge

"Wow, I absolutely love the book. John's anecdotal stories are so engaging."
Sal Randazzo, Retired Educator

"John's keen eye observes then captures images of nature at their finest!"
Phil Krawchuk, Wildlife Naturalist

"The photos and tales John shares spark true joy."
Larissa Grass, Director of Education,
Gallery North

OTHER FICTION BOOKS BY
JOHN P. CARDONE

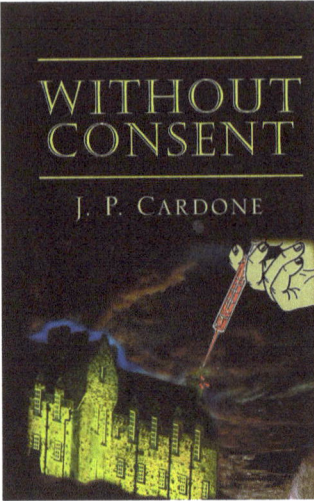

Dr. Elaine Edwards was looking forward to her career as medical director of the Golden Shores Nursing Home. Little did she know she would be thrust into a world of drugs, mystery, and death. She finds herself an unlikely partner to a street-tough, retired New York City detective. Together, they set off to learn why his brother, and other residents at one of Long Island's prestigious nursing homes, ended up suddenly dying. Jason Briggs and his pharmaceutical moguls have other plans and a future filled with greed and selfish wants. It's more than a story about good versus evil, it is a story of compassion versus greed.

"A timely mystery that hits a sweet spot."

Midwest Book Review

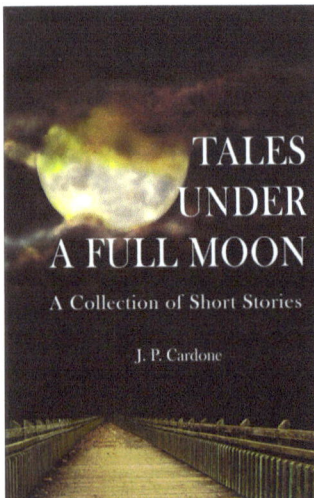

A collection of seven modern day short stories that without a doubt clearly fall under a full moon—when people do act strangely and weird things happen. Escape into the lives of ordinary people, who, for one reason or another, find themselves caught up in the events of the moment. Rich with likable characters oftentimes pushed to their limits, these stories will capture your attention and your heart. While the stories go in one direction, the conclusions always have a twist that will land you in the unexpected.

"Engaging short stories with unique presentations."

ArmchairInterviews.com

"A fun read with some amazing stories."

BookReview.com

To learn more about John's books visit:
www.WaterviewsArts.com

OTHER FICTION BOOKS BY
JOHN P. CARDONE

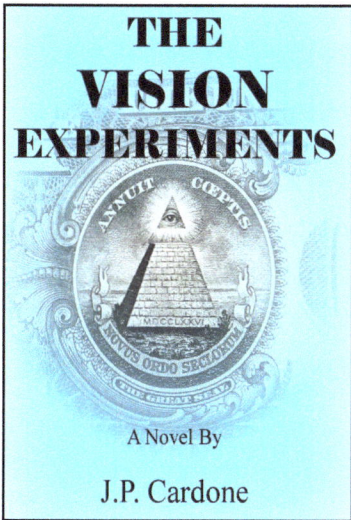

THE VISION EXPERIMENTS

A Novel By

J.P. Cardone

All speech pathologist Dr. Melissa Speyer hoped for was to help her pediatric patient Jason overcome his speech and language difficulties. Instead, she finds herself on a journey where seeing into the future brings new meaning to having a vision. All while her partner, Professor William Clarkson finds himself caught between his love for her and his career ambitions. Enter a wealthy real estate mogul whose desire for fame creates a race to uncover the secrets of history's greats at the expense of innocent people who happen to be in the wrong place at the wrong time. Can two savvy LA Homicide Detectives, with the help of an FBI Agent, uncover the apparent murders of a serial killer or are they distracted by the evidence at hand? *The Vision Experiments* has it all: murder, sex, violence, greed, love, betrayal, and mystery. All in a fast paced, page-turning tale taking place opening in Oxford, England and moving from the coast to coast in the U.S.

"This fast-paced blend of mystery, thriller, and detective story is brimming with curiosity and enthusiasm."
Booklife Reviews

"This is one excellent, mind-grabbing story. A great book!"
Russ Moran, author of The Gray Ship

"An entertaining thriller with a unique premise."
Times Beacon Record Newspapers

To learn more about John's books visit:
www.WaterviewsArts.com

OTHER POETRY BOOKS BY
JEFF RIMLAND

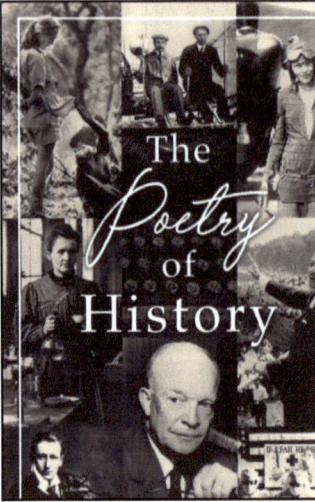

The Poetry of History is unique. It contains photographs, descriptions, and poetry of historical figures and events. The photographs and descriptions are authentic, but the poetry is the author's interpretation and historically accurate. These events and historical figures are placed in chronological order, going as far back in history as 1014 A.D. There have been some key events and key dates that represent so much. Whether it be history taking place thousands of years ago, or taking place in the 20th or 21st century, the events have had an indelible effect on the psyche. No matter what events or historical figures have shown us, we all should try to live by the edict: remember history lest we are doomed to repeat it.

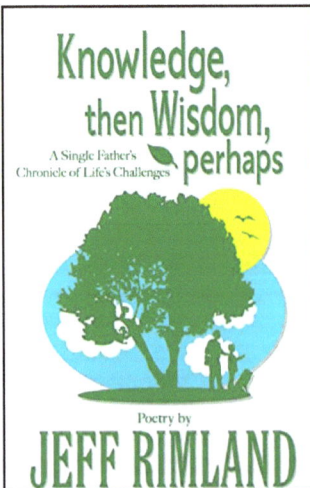

Knowledge, then Wisdom, Perhaps: A Single Father's Chronicle of Life's Challenges details in poetic fashion the various challenges that continually need to be overcome in all of our lives, but has special meaning to single fathers. The population of single parents in the United States is growing every year. As of 2010, the United States Census Bureau estimates that 15% of single parents are men, which translates into 1.8 million single fathers. Single fathers often exist through painful events in their lives such as death of a spouse or divorce. *Knowledge, then Wisdom, Perhaps: A Single Father's Chronicle of Life's Challenges* again is dedicated to all of those single fathers who share pain and hope with the author, but cannot share their feelings.

To learn more about Jeff's books and his poetry visit:
www.ThePoetryOfJeffRimland.com

OTHER POETRY BOOKS BY
JEFF RIMLAND

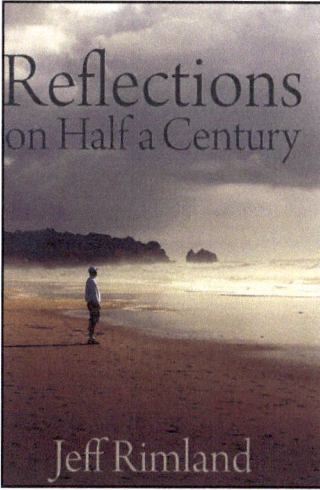

Growing up a "baby boomer" in NY in 1955; through the 50s, 60s, 70s, married in 1977, raising 3 children, working for 30 years, his beloved wife dying in 2001, earning a graduate degree, now a single parent, and his poetry being published are the inspiration behind *Reflections on Half a Century*. Other "baby boomers," a population that numbers over 80 million in 2009, will relate to *Reflections on Half a Century*. This meaningful chapbook chronicles five decades of the author's life, giving rise to emotions that many of us are not able to express in words.

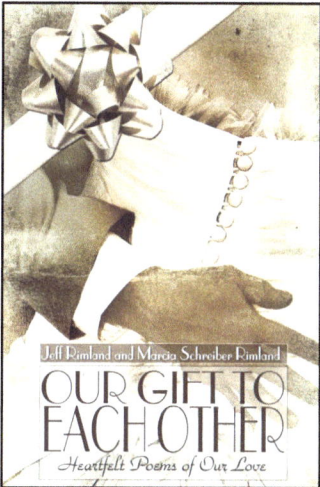

Our Gift to Each Other: Heartfelt Poems of Our Love is Jeff's second book of poetry, coauthored with his wife, Marcia Schreiber Rimland, who passed away from Breast Cancer on October 17, 2001, and is a prequel and linked beautifully to his first book of poetry, *A Widower's Journey: A Life of Loss & Love*.

To learn more about Jeff's books and his poetry visit:
www.ThePoetryOfJeffRimland .com

OTHER POETRY BOOKS BY
JEFF RIMLAND

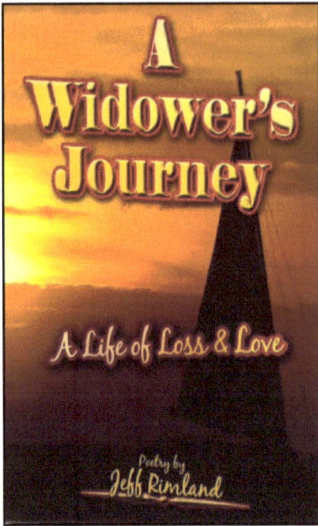

Jeff Rimland's first chapbook of 50 poems, *A Widower's Journey: A Life of Loss & Love,* is a result of many years of authoring about 200 poems, as well as the last 4 years of a life-changing journey, a journey that started by writing down his feelings which he found difficult to express verbally, but is expressed in poems that others can identify with, who have gone through similar experiences. This collection of poetry tells a story of a young man starting out in life, experiencing the beginning of love and relationships, seeking the one true love, finding that love, losing that love due to death, reluctantly accepting that tremendous loss, and finally looking toward the future.

To learn more about Jeff's books and his poetry visit:
www.ThePoetryOfJeffRimland.com

REVIEW NOTES: